YOUR NEXT ELEVEN MARKETING MOVES

Proven strategies that can help you **get found** and **stand out** in the chaos.

ROBERT JOHN HADFIELD

YOUR NEXT ELEVEN MARKETING MOVES

Proven strategies that can help you get found and stand out in the chaos.

© 2024 Robert John Hadfield. All rights reserved.

No part of this book may be reproduced, distributed, or transmitted in any form or by any means, including recording, photocopying, or other electronic or mechanical methods, without the prior written permission of the Robert John Hadfield, except in the case of brief quotations embodied in critical reviews and certain other noncommercial uses permitted by copyright law. For permission requests, write to the publisher, addressed "Attention: Permissions Coordinator," at the address below or using the contact form at thickandmystic.com.

Robert John Hadfield
Thick and Mystic Media, LLC
955 North 1300 West, Suite #14
St. George, UT 84770

Please purchase only authorized editions and do not participate in or encourage piracy of copyrighted materials. Your support of the author's rights is appreciated.

thickandmystic.com
audiomover.com
robertjohnhadfield.com

Written by Robert John Hadfield
Editing Assistance by Robert Dean Hadfield

Paperback ISBN: 9798332511806
Hard Cover ISBN: 9798332969942

Also available as an Audiobook

thickandmystic

Thank you to Rebecca for continually motivating me to raise my standards.

SETTING THE STAGE

Throughout this book I am going to reference an organization called Audiomover. Audiomover is a company I started in a home recording studio in my basement in 2000. Its primary service is converting audio and video tapes to digital.

From its humble beginnings in my home in Thornton, CO, Audiomover grew into a nationally-known, respected and profitable company.

Audiomover was one of the early companies to truly utilize the power of the Internet and the small world it created. In our niche, we mastered search engines and capitalized on turning the entire country into our market. I mastered Search Engine Optimization (SEO) before most people had ever heard the term and we quickly gained customers from coast to coast.

Like so many other Internet-based companies, we developed a significant national footprint without having a national physical presence.

Through its history Audiomover worked on projects for major universities, government agencies (city, county, state and federal), well-known musicians and musical groups, major religious institutions, media organizations, historical preservation societies, famous authors and artists, and countless numbers of families and individuals across the United States and Canada.

We worked on one record-setting project in which we converted 115,000 cassette tapes to digital for a single client. We were even involved in digitizing historical recordings for a former Vice President of the United States.

The growth and continued success of Audiomover is the result of effectively using the marketing strategies and philosophies I will share in this book.

Amazingly, Audiomover's growth was achieved with almost no formal advertising. In the two and a half decades Audiomover has been in business, we have spent less than $5,000 advertising our services. It's an amazing fact when you consider the disproportionately large impact we had on that niche industry.

Although I don't recommend *not advertising* as a strategy, our success shows how applying correct marketing techniques and principles can lead to a thriving business - even one with a small advertising/marketing budget.

The strategies I used to build Audiomover are the foundation of this book. They can be applied to small, one-person businesses as well as large corporations. The ideas are easy to implement and will help you grow your company in the midst of the noise in any industry. The ideas and principles will not be a perfect fit for every business, but they can be modified for almost any business that seeks to build its audience and customer base.

Building Audiomover puts me in a unique position as a marketing and media consultant. Unlike many marketing specialists who utilize other people's money to experiment and develop strategies, I used my own company and resources to develop my craft. The bottom line is, the marketing strategies I discuss in this book have been tried and tested and proven to generate success.

It is very likely that most people reading this book have never heard some of the ideas I am going to share with you. Some of them I have never shared beyond the companies I directly consult with. And others are unique twists on more common ideas explaining how you can use them in your unique situation.

Several of these strategies were developed in response to solving challenging marketing problems experienced at Audiomover. Others revealed themselves as happy accidents, the kind that often appear in the process of focused work.

As you read this book, I think you will notice that most of the strategies seem not only novel but obvious. And with a little creativity, the strategies can be modified for use in almost any organization, taking it to a higher level and beyond.

FIGURING IT OUT

I earned a Bachelor's Degree in Advertising in the mid-nineties. Although I was enamored with the creative visual and written aspects of advertising, it became obvious that being creative in that way wasn't enough to be successful in advertising. Long-term success in advertising requires a great amount of critical data. And gathering data requires some level of experimentation. And experimentation has traditionally required money.

A major challenge with advertising is that the number of variables in the data is broad and deep. The variables in a simple print ad can be overwhelming to track and manage. In a print ad, for example variables can include the copy, the artwork, the message, the size, the placement, the timing, the reach, the frequency and the demographics, just to name some of the more obvious. And the success or failure of a print ad can be tied to a single variable, a combination of variables, or even some variable you aren't aware of.

Managing these variables and doing the necessary experiments over a long enough period are reasonable for massive corporate entities. But **most businesses don't have the time or resources to do this**. So the majority of companies find themselves in the world of **guess, spend and hope** when it comes to advertising.

As I finished my degree I was actually pretty discouraged about the whole thing. Especially having started some small businesses myself in high school and watching my own father build a successful company from the ground up. I understood the world of budgets and limited resources, and it seemed as though my newly-acquired degree would have limited value in the majority of the business world.

Little did I know that the rise of the Internet would be an equalizer that would create a new strategic playing field – one that I would benefit from dramatically.

I started my first marketing job in January 2000 as a marketing coordinator for a small engineering firm. And although we developed traditional advertising materials like print ads and mailers, we also developed new things like multimedia presentations, online training tools, interactive CDs and web pages.

THE RISE OF SEO

Search Engine Optimization (SEO) was a relatively new concept in those days, and it became my primary focus early on.

By 2000, millions of people were either online, or coming online each year. So the challenge we faced was, *how do we get the people searching for our service to visit our web site without our direct intervention?*

This was an important question because getting people to visit your web site was often an effort of traditional advertising methods. We sent mailers and created print ads in the physical world to get people to visit us in the digital world. Considering that platforms like Google and Yahoo! were, for all intents and purposes, free, our efforts changed. We became highly-focused on getting found through customer searches rather than depending on the guesswork of traditional advertising.

I spent a lot of time pouring over graphs, charts and raw data mastering the skill of SEO.

By 2002 I had mastered many of the principles and gained enough experience to open my own marketing and media firm. I called it "Thick and Mystic Media" (a name borrowed from a publishing company I had started years earlier).

Over the next few years I worked with companies and individuals throughout the Denver metro area. I helped a variety of organizations develop marketing strategies and utilize all of the new tools that were rapidly entering the marketplace.

And at the same time, I started applying those same skills to Audiomover (the company discussed in the first part of this book). And Audiomover quickly established a meaningful footprint across the country.

THE PPC REVOLUTION

Around 2004 an associate of mine who owned an advertising agency offered me a ticket to a seminar hosted by Yahoo! The seminar was about a relatively new concept called pay-per-click (PPC) advertising.

Attending this seminar was a turning point for Audiomover and for me personally.

PPC was a miracle for me - someone who was so pessimistic about paid advertising for small companies. It all but solved the **guess, spend and hope** problem with traditional advertising. PPC created a direct connection between an advertiser and a pre-qualified customer.

I vividly remember walking out of the seminar with an excitement I had rarely felt before. Although PPC didn't replace SEO, it dramatically streamlined it; like moving from a bicycle to a jet.

And while SEO cost nothing, at the time PPC cost little more than nothing.

If you are not familiar with the generic concept of PPC, it is a tool that eventually evolved into **Adwords** and now **Google Ads**. In the early days, it was simply a text "ad" that would appear at the very top of a search results page. It actually didn't look any different than other search results, so very few people at the time realized they were ads.

For example, if you search on the term "Tire Store," in a Google search box, the very first result displayed will likely be a link to a local tire store. The tire store on that link is literally paying to be at the top of the results. That specific tire store had previously selected the range of words and phrases it wanted to be found on. Then it placed a bid to appear at the top of the list whenever someone searched on one of those terms. Today you can identify those "ads" because they have the word "Sponsored" next to them.

Among other things, PPC had two game-changing features:

1. *You could advertise directly to a person who searched on a specific search term. It was a*

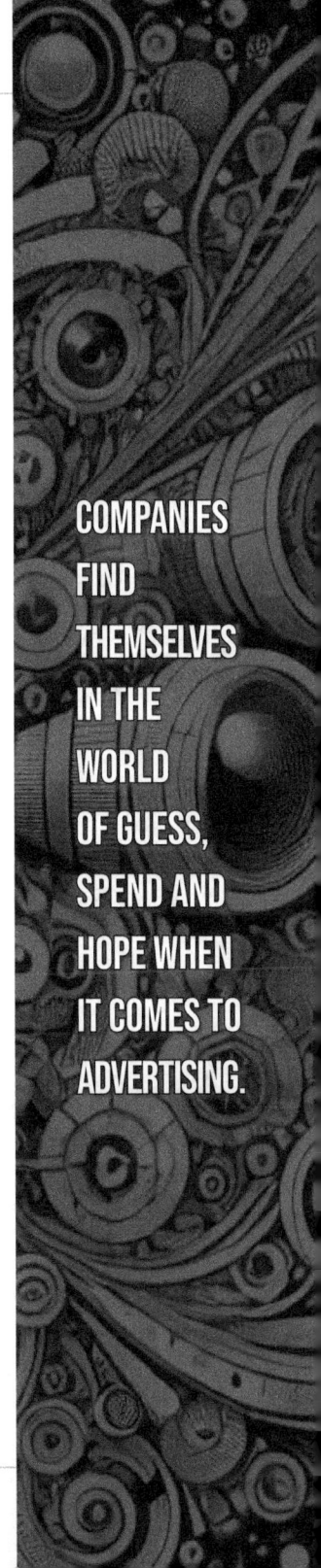

COMPANIES FIND THEMSELVES IN THE WORLD OF GUESS, SPEND AND HOPE WHEN IT COMES TO ADVERTISING.

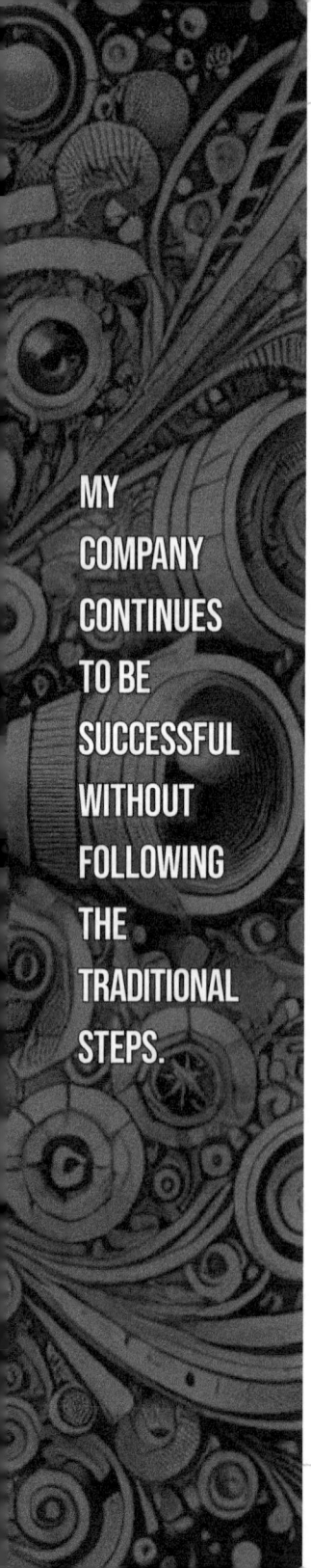

MY COMPANY CONTINUES TO BE SUCCESSFUL WITHOUT FOLLOWING THE TRADITIONAL STEPS.

high-tech way of pre-qualifying a customer.

2. *You didn't have to pay for the ad unless someone clicked on it. Thus the generic name pay-per-click.*

After the seminar I immediately implemented several PPC campaigns for Audiomover. We targeted search terms and phrases like "Convert cassette to CD," "Transfer cassette to digital" and "Audio tape to digital."

Back then each click was only a few pennies. And because Audiomover was one of the only companies offering the digitizing service, it was normal for us to only spend $0.25 a day on PPC advertising.

To this day, PPC remains the only formal advertising we've ever used for Audiomover.

THE EVOLUTION OF PPC

Eventually, a number of large companies like Walgreen's, Costco and Kodak, along with dozens of smaller start-up companies, began moving into Audiomover's space. As a result, PPC advertising became more expensive. Keywords that once cost only a few pennies now cost several dollars. So eventually I stopped using it altogether.

Amazingly, Audiomover continues to thrive today with no advertising effort on my part. The orders have never stopped even though we haven't actively advertised our services in over a decade.

As you read this book you will understand why Audiomover continues to be successful without following the traditional advertising steps, and you will have the knowledge to do the same thing yourself.

I said this before and it is worth repeating. ***I don't suggest not advertising as a strategy.*** It's likely we would have experienced even more success had I put the time, effort and money into formally advertising the business.

So this book is not intended to be a resource for doing things cheaply. However, if you don't have a lot of money to spend promoting your business, the tools in this book will be very helpful to you. But if you do have money to spend promoting your business, the tools in this book will enable you to take your business to even greater heights.

SEARCH AND AI

As noted, I have been involved with SEO in one form or another since the year 2000, and one thing is clear: no one knows the exact algorithm used by search engines such as Google. A decade ago it was common for marketing companies to claim they knew how to work the algorithm. They didn't. And it's the same today as it was then. We can make guesses based on our experience, but the algorithm is unclear and may be constantly changing.

But here is what you need to know. ***Search engines and AI (Artificial Intelligence) are in the business of providing reliable and useful information***. Everything in this book will have a better chance of working if you or your company provide high-quality information. Don't try to take short cuts or trick the system. These tools and strategies work best when you give the search engine what it wants. What does it want? It wants to ***provide the best possible answers and information to the people conducting searches***. So its up to you to provide that.

As you review the principles outlined in this book, please understand: nothing works well 100% of the time. Google's indexing is unpredictable so you can't ever be certain.

However, the strategies I will outline in this book can and will work. But they may not work the first time you apply them. Then again, they might. You are at the mercy of the search engine algorithms and timing. But because these strategies are built on marketing principles (not tricks) and cost little or nothing to implement, you can experiment with them with minimal impact on your bottom line.

EMBRACE YOUTUBE

One of the biggest challenges I face when dealing with new clients is their **lack of understanding** of the value of YouTube as a marketing tool.

When I begin working with a client, I often hear a refrain that goes something like this:

"My customers aren't looking for us on YouTube,"

- or -

"People don't search for our services on YouTube."

While those statements may be technically true, they reflect a fundamental misunderstanding of SEO, video content and the broad value of YouTube. Video is fundamental to marketing today and YouTube is foundational as a platform for communication and messaging strategies.

Understanding the six principles described on the next few pages will help you understand the strategies outlined in the rest of the book.

Please Note: While much of this book is focused on ideas for creating meaningful and strategic video content, I am not going to discuss strategies behind creating YouTube thumbnails. While unique thumbnails are not necessary, they can play an important role in how people respond to your video. There are many tools available to help you create them and, if possible, I recommend creating a specific thumbnail for each video you post on YouTube.

1. GOOGLE AND YOUTUBE INTEGRATION

Google is the world's most popular search engine, and YouTube is the second. Google owns YouTube, and their integration is seamless. When a user searches for something on Google, the search engine aims to provide the most comprehensive results possible, which often includes videos. If you use Google, you have probably noticed that it integrates YouTube video results alongside text results in its search results pages.

Having videos on YouTube related to your business significantly increases your chances of being found on Google searches. Even if your web page doesn't show up in search results, your videos often do, and vice versa. In some cases, having videos will double or triple the number of times your business shows up in the first set of Google results.

2. A LIBRARY, NOT A TIMELINE

Unlike Facebook or Instagram, which operate as timelines, YouTube operates as a library. Content on platforms such as Facebook and Instagram has a short lifespan. If you've ever had someone *Like* or *Comment* on one of your older posts on Facebook – for example, a vacation photo you posted three years ago – it seems a little weird.

This is completely different on YouTube. YouTube videos have an indefinite lifespan, and can provide value for years. With regard to Audiomover, some videos I posted many years ago continue to generate business. This means that content created today can remain relevant and beneficial for years to come. A video you post today, which gains very few views, might just take off and get thousands of views two years from now. I've seen this happen. Posting a video, whatever the immediate result, is rarely a waste of time.

3. NUMBERS DON'T MATTER

Don't get hung up on the number of views or followers you have on YouTube, unless your goal is to monetize your channel through ad revenue or sponsorships. Instead, focus on creating highly-targeted videos with good information. Even if a video only gets a handful of views, if you do it right, most of those views will come from pre-qualified potential customers.

Each video is like a fishing hook; the more hooks you have in the water, the greater your chances of catching a fish. Every strategically created video increases your chances of being discovered by the right audience, whether it's today or ten years from now.

Thinking of YouTube as a library of valuable content rather than a platform for immediate views will shift your focus to creating useful videos.

The more specific and targeted you can be, the better your results will be. Think of each video the exact opposite way you think of traditional advertising media. When using traditional advertising, one advertisement has to appeal to thousands of people. On the other hand, when using YouTube, each video can be targeted to a very small group

NOTE: While my primary focus here is on YouTube, it's worth mentioning that TikTok shares a similar non-timeline characteristic. This makes it another valuable platform for creating long-lasting content that brings in potential customers well into the future.

4. YOUTUBE TRANSCRIPTIONS

Another critical feature of YouTube is its automatic transcription. YouTube transcribes every video, making all the speaking in your videos searchable text. This means that Google search results frequently include sections of videos where specific questions are answered, even if the description, the hash tags and the title don't mention them. This enhances your content's discoverability.

It goes without saying that the more videos you create, the more searchable text you will have for people looking for your product or service. This enables Google to tie your service to various search terms by indexing the words spoken in the video. As a result, each video serves as a stand-alone piece of content and enriches your overall SEO strategy. It does this by increasing the amount of indexed content related to your business.

5. MUSIC

Many years ago I was listening to a talk by a famous composer who said, "The only problem with real life is it doesn't have background music."

Music is he easiest and fastest way to connect with another person on an emotional level. Every great film maker understands this. I'm sure you've noticed that a well-produced TV Spot or advertisement can take you on an emotional journey, and maybe even bring a tear to your eye in only 30 seconds.

Advertisements accomplish that with strategic music.

Sadly, there isn't a practical (or non-weird) way to add background music to meetings and sales calls.

But creating videos gives you an opportunity to attach the powerful tool of music to any marketing message. Whether your message is light-hearted, funny, somber, exciting, or motivating, videos enable you to attach your message to music. Great film makers, advertisers, marketers and storytellers understand the power of music, and making videos gives you the opportunity to harness that power.

Music can help your product or service resonate with your customers in a way only music can. It can take a good video and make it amazing.

6. "HERE I GO AGAIN" STRATEGY

If you were around in 1987 you remember the hit song, "Here I Go Again" by the British band Whitesnake. The song hit number one in the U.S., and was in constant rotation on radio and MTV.

More than any other song they recorded, it put Whitesnake on the map and almost single-handedly made them a headlining act. Today that song still ranks up there near Bon Jovi's "Living on a Prayer" as an 80s anthem, and you just might hear it at your local Karaoke night this weekend.

What most people don't realize is that when they released that song in 1987, it was their second attempt. Whitesnake had previously recorded and released that song five years earlier in 1982 on a different album. But no one noticed. It didn't even chart in the US, let alone reach number one.

If you listen to the two recordings back to back, they are very similar. No one can say exactly what it was, but some simple tweaks and a re-release changed that song from a disappointment into the biggest song in the world. And because of that, you gotta love the fact that the song itself is called, "Here I Go Again."

What's the point? YouTube gives you the freedom to use this same strategy. If you post a video and it doesn't go anywhere, make some adjustments and post it again (and again and again). There is no need to release brand new stuff every time you make a video. If you think a video is good and the content is valuable, keep modifying it and posting it until it works. Unlike the 1980s, in today's world of media, you can even delete the old version as if it never existed - or not.

Creating new videos can take a lot of time and energy. But modifying old videos is pretty easy.

Not every piece of media needs to be a fresh idea. Just ask Whitesnake.

VIDEO ROBERT'S RULES to REMEMBER

1. MICROPHONE

Use a **good microphone** that's placed **close to you**. Mics on phones and computers are great, but they still can't replace a good external microphone.

Bad audio can ruin good video. People will turn off a good movie if the sound is bad. People will treat your videos the same way.

2. SUBTITLES

Add subtitles. Many people scroll social media with the sound off, without subtitles they will skip your video. And even with the sound on, people are more likely to watch your video if it has subtitles.

3. LIGHTING

Make sure you are **well lit from the front**. Lights above you (room lights) create shadows that make your eyes dark. People will be more confident in you if your eyes are bright and clear.

4. MUSIC

Add background music. Good music can dramatically amplify your message. If you took the music out of your favorite movies you would likely be bored with them.

Also, make sure your background music doesn't overpower your voice. It should be slightly quieter than you think it needs to be.

5. SETTING

Don't film with a window behind you unless it's covered, especially if you can see the sky. It will almost always blow out the shot and make it difficult to see you clearly.

READ IT OUT LOUD

*How to dramatically **increase** the **value** of customer testimonials.*

CORE CONCEPTS AND PRINCIPLES FOR SUCCESS:

- Showcase your passion to attract people.
- Present testimonials personally.
- Use music to amplify your message.
- Create keyword-rich and search-friendly content.

In the early days of Audiomover, I recognized the importance of collecting customer testimonials. Every time we sent digitized tapes back to our customers, we included a note asking them to share a testimonial with us. And whenever we received a testimonial, we would post it in various areas on our website.

As I reviewed our web stats, I realized that people often take additional steps to find customer reviews. I noticed that many people search for testimonials as part of a Google search. I even do this in my own life. If I am interested in doing business with a particular company, or researching a product, I will frequently do a Google search for testimonials and reviews for the product or service.

As it related to Audiomover, I noticed that people frequently conduct web searches on phrases like "Audiomover Customer Testimonials" and "Audiomover Review" and even things as broad as, "Is Audiomover Any Good?"

A few years ago, I had an experience that helped me recognize a new way of benefiting from this common practice.

One day we received a handwritten note in the mail from a customer expressing heartfelt thanks for the wonderful job we did converting a tape to digital. I took the note and read it to one of the employees in our studio, commenting how nice it was to receive something so complimentary. Then it dawned on me - **we should be filming this moment.**

With this thought in mind, we set up a spot in our studio where we could film ourselves reading customer testimonials.

I printed several of the best testimonials we received. I thought it would look more organic and personal reading from paper than reading from a phone or tablet. I sat down in front of a camera, hit record and started reading them one by one.

I began each video with an introduction that included where the testimonial came from; e.g., "We received this customer testimonial from Pennsylvania." I then read the testimonial out loud, pausing occasionally to elaborate on interesting points the customer made and describe how specific things in the testimonial related to our business practices.

At the end of each testimonial, I acknowledged the customer by name, thanked them for their feedback, and shared additional thoughts on what they said. At the end of each video I invited anyone watching or listening to consider utilizing our services.

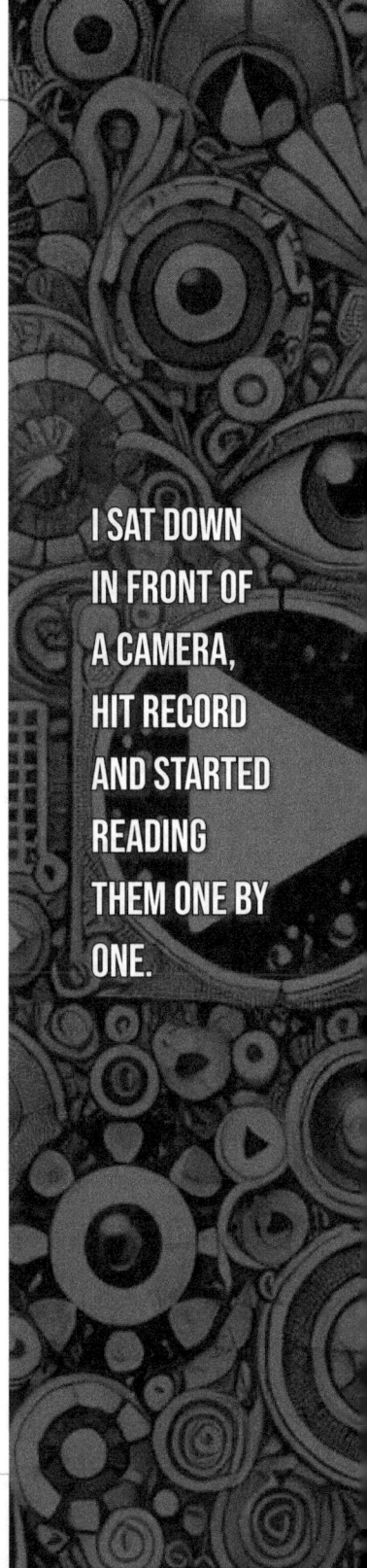

I SAT DOWN IN FRONT OF A CAMERA, HIT RECORD AND STARTED READING THEM ONE BY ONE.

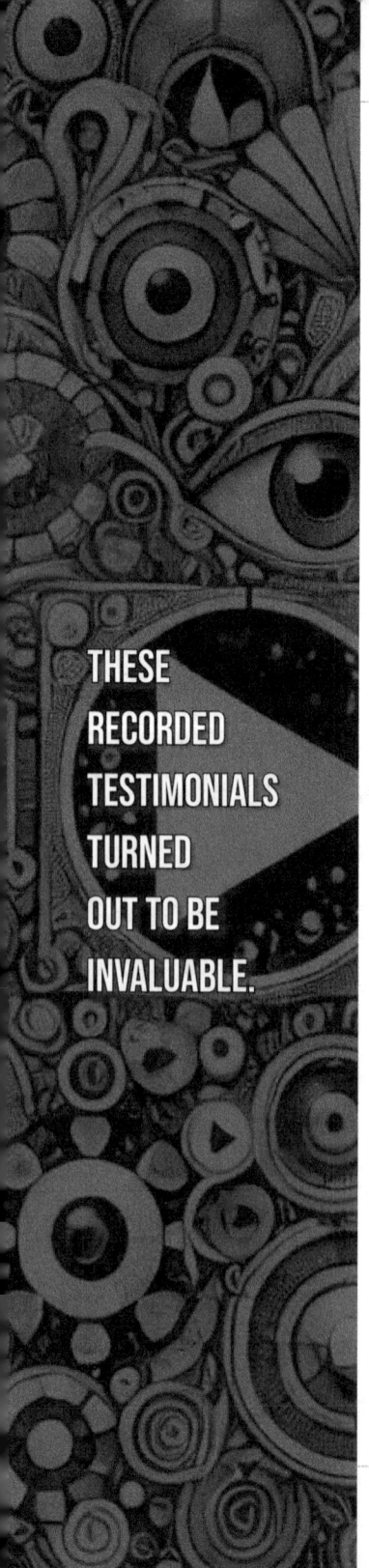

THESE RECORDED TESTIMONIALS TURNED OUT TO BE INVALUABLE.

These recorded testimonials turned out to be invaluable. We shot them from different angles using high quality cameras, lighting, and sound equipment. The videos were visually engaging and emotionally compelling. When we added background music, many of the testimonials became real tear-jerkers, especially those where customers shared tender feelings about family members who had passed on and whose emotions had been awakened by our services.

We posted the testimonials on our YouTube channel. We also gave each video a unique title that corresponded to search words and phrases we had seen in the data, such as, "Audiomover Customer Testimonial," "Audiomover Review," and "Audiomover Customer Success Story."

In order to ensure a broader reach, no two titles were the same.

Many people who call our office comment on watching the testimonials and have even expressed that it played a role in why they chose our company to service their needs.

WHAT TO DO:

- *Print your best customer testimonials.*
- *Film yourself reading them.*
- *Make one video for each testimonial.*
- *Include personal comments and insights about the items in the testimonial.*
- *Thank the customer for the kind words.*
- *Invite viewers to use your service.*
- *Add background music.*
- *Post the videos to your YouTube channel.*
- *Create unique titles for each video that correspond to common search phrases.*
- *Include the videos on your web site.*

PEOPLE ALSO ASK

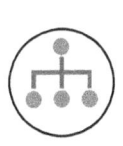 *Use Google's **People Also Ask** section for **limitless content** ideas.*

CORE CONCEPTS AND PRINCIPLES FOR SUCCESS:

- Demonstrate your expertise to built trust.
- Produce a large quantity of content.
- Use Google to generate ideas.
- Generate search-friendly topics and titles.

One day several years ago, while performing a routine Google search, I came across something that inspired the inception of another marketing strategy. As I scrolled down the "Google results" page, a small section entitled "People also ask" caught my eye. This section featured a list of questions related to my search.

This was a list of searches that other people had performed that were similar to my search. Google was using an AI to help me fine tune my own search.

I instantly recognized it as a tool for my business. I realized that if I performed searches related to Audiomover in a Google search box, the "People also ask" section would give me insight into my potential customers' behavior and language.

I realized I could learn a great deal about what was running through our customers' minds. The questions I searched on not only spawned more questions in the "People also ask" section, but they included phrases and terminology our customers use most often.

It was clear to me that if we could tap into this resource, it would provide an almost **never-ending supply of material to create effective and relevant videos**.

Similar to the customer testimonial videos mentioned previously, we set up another spot in our studio where we could record "People also ask" videos. One team member managed the camera, another team member sat with a laptop and a Google search page open, and I stood in front of the camera.

The team member managing the Google search page would type the search phrase in Google. He would then read aloud each question in the "People also ask" section. Next, I would look into the camera, state the question and answer it off the cuff. I didn't need a script because I knew our services inside and out. I addressed each question as if I were talking directly to a customer.

In the process of the recordings we uncovered questions that had never crossed our minds. One of the most surprising questions was, "Does Costco convert tapes to digital?" It was a question I never would have considered, but there it was, straight from the mouths of our potential customers. Google was literally telling me that some of my potential customers were searching on this phrase.

So I looked in the camera, I repeated this "Costco" question, and then answered it. I explained that while Costco

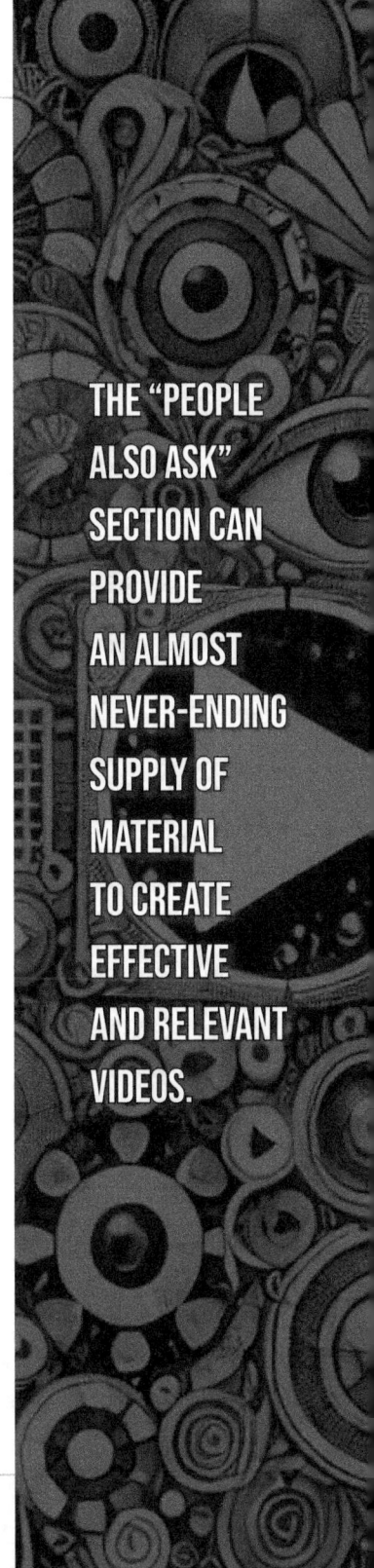

THE "PEOPLE ALSO ASK" SECTION CAN PROVIDE AN ALMOST NEVER-ENDING SUPPLY OF MATERIAL TO CREATE EFFECTIVE AND RELEVANT VIDEOS.

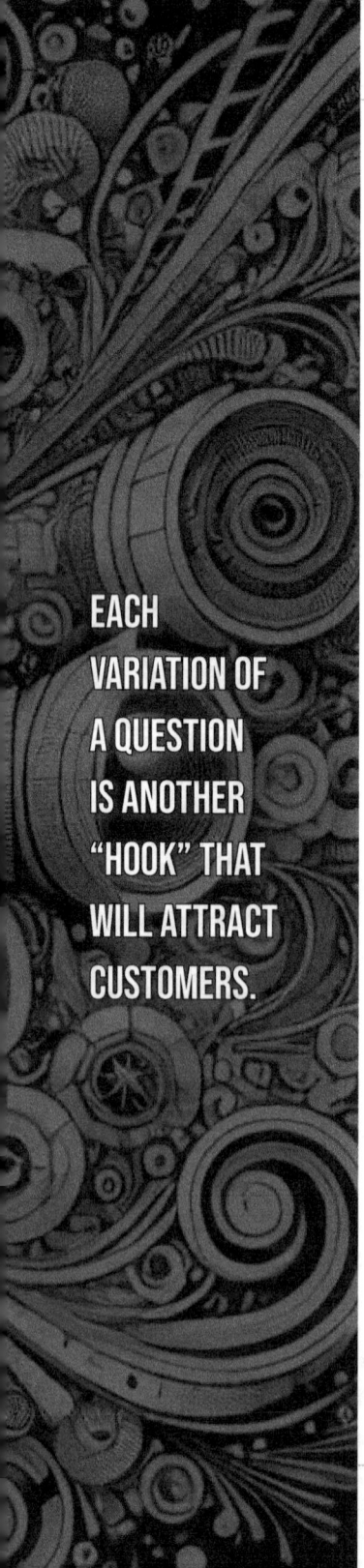

> EACH VARIATION OF A QUESTION IS ANOTHER "HOOK" THAT WILL ATTRACT CUSTOMERS.

offers a digitizing service, Audiomover provides a more attentive service. I emphasized the value of customers knowing who would be handling their treasured memories, and contrasted our hands-on approach to the anonymous approach used by big-box stores.

That Costco video has garnered thousands of views. And amazingly, we have received numerous phone calls and orders from people who have watched that video.

In one particularly memorable call the customer said, "I just saw a commercial that said I should use you guys instead of Costco to digitize my tapes."

Of course we had not made any commercials. What the man saw was our YouTube video. And because it was recorded so well, he assumed it was some sort of TV commercial.

I would have never thought of asking, "Does Costco convert tapes to digital?" if I had not looked in the "People also ask" section. And I certainly wouldn't have created a video to address it.

As you use this strategy, you will find that many questions overlap. Use them anyway because each variation of a question is another "hook" that will attract customers. Remember, you can insert different keywords, descriptions and titles, all of which are good for Google searches. And if you answer these questions off-script, you are likely to say things slightly different, which will create more keyword-rich content.

These videos, created at minimal expense, have become powerful marketing tools for our business. They have answered critical questions, built trust with our customers, and improved our visibility on Google.

The success of these videos can be found in their simplicity: we listened to our customers and spoke their language. By addressing their questions, we not only boosted our SEO but established ourselves as trustworthy, knowledgeable business people who gave them the information and confidence they needed to make good decisions.

WHAT TO DO:

- *Conduct a Google search related to your business.*
- *Scroll down to the "People also ask" results.*
- *Read one of the questions into the camera **exactly as it is written**, then answer it.*
- *Make one video for each question. Don't worry if questions are similar, do them anyway.*

- *Add background music.*
- *Post the videos to your YouTube channel.*
- *Create titles for each video that match the "People Also Ask" question exactly.*
- *You can even create a separate page for each video on your web site. Embed the video on the page and use the transcript to create the text for the page. Plug the transcript into an AI and it will generate a nice overview.*

HOW TO VIDEOS

Engage and build trust using behind-the-scenes informative videos.

CORE CONCEPTS AND PRINCIPLES FOR SUCCESS:

- Leverage routine tasks to create content.
- Establish credibility by demonstrating skills.
- Utilize SEO strategies in titles and descriptions.
- Captivate viewers with behind-the-scenes content.

At Audiomover, our primary service is converting audio and video tapes into digital formats. We often receive libraries consisting of thousands of tapes. Inevitably, some of the tapes are broken.

Over the years repairing tapes has become a significant part of our operation. And even though many repairs are similar, no two are identical. We actually have a box of special tools and spare parts to help us make those repairs.

Nearly ten years ago, I had an idea. It struck me that people might find the process of repairing a cassette tape interesting. Drawing inspiration from shows like "How It's Made" and "Bob Ross's painting sessions," I wondered if there might be a group of people who would enjoy just sitting and watching a cassette tape being repaired.

At that time, the thought of people enjoying that type of content was less obvious than it is today. Nonetheless, I decided to film myself repairing a cassette tape. I set up a camera above the tape to ensure every detail was visible and I narrated the procedure step by step. To my surprise, the video garnered over 1,000 views within a few months. To date it has garnered over 40,000 views. In addition to the views, it has achieved something else far more valuable - it has established me as an expert in the field of cassette tapes and analog media.

Prospective customers saw the care I put into the repairs, which reinforced my credibility, generated more customer engagement, and increased the number of phone calls and orders we have received.

One customer, the pastor of a church with nearly 1,000 tapes of recorded sermons he needed digitized, watched several of our YouTube videos. What he saw convinced him we were the best organization to handle his tape digitizing project. He was hesitant to mail the tapes, however, fearing they might get lost or damaged in transit. As a result, he drove from California to our studio in Colorado bringing his boxes of tapes with him.

While driving from California to Colorado, the pastor drove past several companies that could have completed his project for him. But when he dropped the tapes off he specifically referenced the repair videos we made. He said that he had watched the videos and could tell that I had the knowledge, passion and experience he wanted for his important project. That little connection is why he felt comfortable driving nearly a thousand miles and dropping his project off with us.

This experience taught me an im-

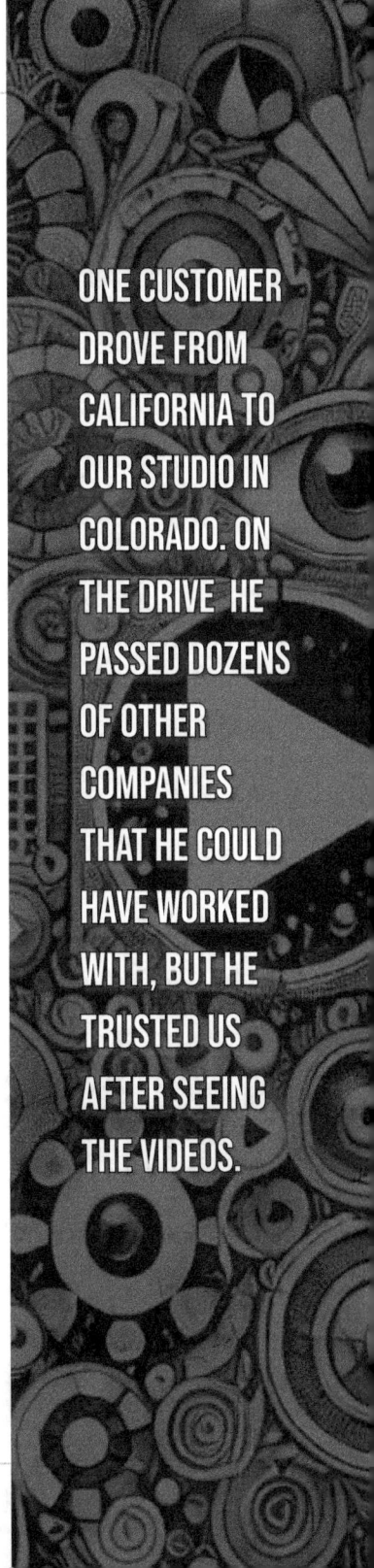

ONE CUSTOMER DROVE FROM CALIFORNIA TO OUR STUDIO IN COLORADO. ON THE DRIVE HE PASSED DOZENS OF OTHER COMPANIES THAT HE COULD HAVE WORKED WITH, BUT HE TRUSTED US AFTER SEEING THE VIDEOS.

EVERY BIT OF CONTENT YOU CREATE STRENGTHENS YOUR POSITION AS AN EXPERT IN YOUR FIELD AND HELPS POTENTIAL CUSTOMERS FIND YOU.

portant lesson: what might seem mundane or routine to one person could be very intriguing to another. Maybe even act as the closer in a sale.

In your business, you probably have some tasks that seem mundane or insignificant. On the other hand, those tasks might captivate the attention of another person or group of people and position you as an expert in your field. For example, consider one of the customers I consult. They operate a facility where they build assorted pieces of furniture. Every time I visit them, they are performing interesting tasks that require unique tools and equipment. When I asked the owner why they never film any of the furniture being built, he said, "I don't think anybody would be interested in watching what we do."

Of course I had to firmly correct him.

Think about all the tasks you perform throughout the day. These tasks have the potential of being topics of interesting videos. Don't discount anything.

As you film tasks being performed and post them on various sites, you will not only drive traffic to your website, you will increase your online presence and establish yourself as a critical player in your industry.

Also, don't be afraid to share your secrets. I have found that if people are determined to do something themselves, they will, whether you show them or not. But more importantly, I have also found that showing how something is done can increase the likelihood of someone using your service. I have received many phone calls over the years where the customer said, "I watched your video and I was planning to do it myself, but after seeing your expertise, I think I would rather pay you to do it."

Take advantage of every opportunity to showcase your expertise. Remember, every bit of content you create strengthens your position as an expert in your field and helps potential customers find you so they can purchase your product or service.

The expertise people witnessed in my repair videos established me as an expert in the field of cassette tapes. I was even invited to be a guest speaker at the "Making Vinyl" conference in Los Angeles in 2019 after the organizer had watched some of our videos.

The simple act of showing others the process your organization uses to generate revenue can become a powerful tool that enhances meaningful engagement and increases your sales.

WHAT TO DO:

- *Consider everything you do behind the scenes as a potential "how to" video. Don't discount anything.*
- *Set up a camera and film yourself doing it.*
- *Make sure you have good audio and talk through the work, explaining each step, even if it seems obvious.*
- *Share jargon and explain what it means.*
- *If possible, add the steps as text on the screen.*
- *Post the video to your YouTube channel.*
- *Create titles that are very specific to the actions in the video. Make sure you use keywords that people will look for. Be careful using jargon in your titles that potential customers won't be looking for.*

SOLVING A MYSTERY

 *Attract customers by sharing something that most people don't know.*

CORE CONCEPTS AND PRINCIPLES FOR SUCCESS:

- Build trust as an expert.
- Play on people's love of learning new things.
- Share institutional knowledge.
- Benefit from the principle of giving before asking.

At Audiomover, we work with fascinating equipment. And because of the nature of our business, much of the equipment is retro in nature. And among our collection of machines is an eight-track tape player.

An eight-track tape was a popular consumer music format during a period when cassettes were coming into prominence. An eight-track tape was nothing more than a cartridge that contained a single spool of audio tape. Although it was short-lived, at one time it was a very popular format for music distribution. And almost anyone who was alive during the 70s and 80s era would be familiar with the eight-track tape format.

Just for fun, one day I asked a member of my staff if he knew why an eight-track tape was called an eight-track tape.

He didn't know.

It occurred to me that many people probably didn't know. I began asking friends and acquaintances the same question and not a single person knew the answer, but they all suddenly wanted to know.

This universal lack of knowledge, and instant curiosity, inspired me to create a video that answered the question.

I set up a camera, brought out the eight-track player and an eight-track tape and started creating a video that would explain the origin of the name "eight-track tape." I spent four or five hours on this project, ensuring the content was informative and engaging. I included detailed graphics to clearly illustrate the concepts.

That video, titled "Why is an Eight-Track Tape Called an Eight-Track Tape?" has garnered approximately 70,000 views on YouTube. If you search for the phrase, "Why is an eight-track tape called an eight-track tape?" on Google, there is a very strong possibility my video will be the first result you see.

This video does more than just educate clients; it reinforces me as an expert in the field of analog media. It also attracts my demographic - an older audience, familiar with eight-track tapes. The same audience that is likely to have media that needs to be converted to digital.

Knowing that those people who view our video are likely to be in my target demographic, I felt it was a subtle way to introduce myself and talk about our business. In the video description I included a link to our website that shares important information about who we are and what we do. In retrospect, I

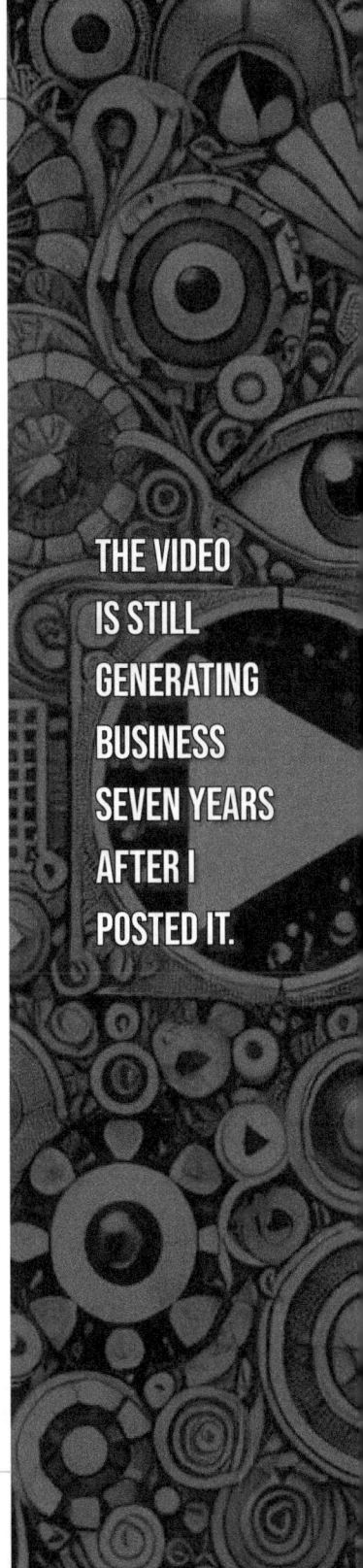

THE VIDEO IS STILL GENERATING BUSINESS SEVEN YEARS AFTER I POSTED IT.

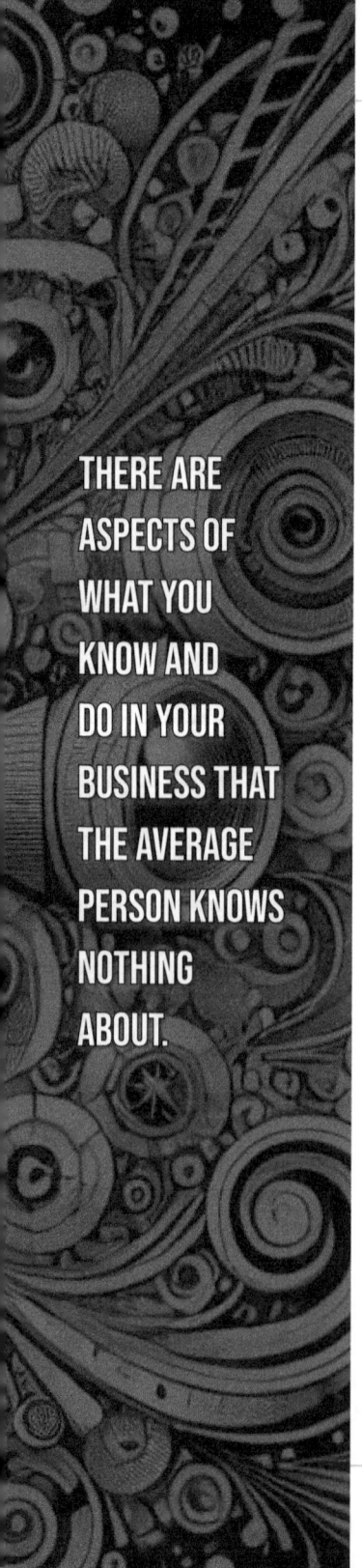

> THERE ARE ASPECTS OF WHAT YOU KNOW AND DO IN YOUR BUSINESS THAT THE AVERAGE PERSON KNOWS NOTHING ABOUT.

could have been a little more assertive with my sales pitch at the end of the video. Even so, the video has still generated many web inquiries, phone calls and orders.

The video follows the Gary Vaynerchuk philosophy of creating content that provides something of value before you ask for something in return. The video entertained and informed the audience who in turn were more interested in working with me.

A number of months ago, I was in the waiting room of a doctor's office watching a TV as it played "How It's Made" videos over and over. When I went to the examination room, I asked the doctor about the TV and videos. He told me something surprising: he said that sometimes patients are so engrossed in the videos they hesitate going to the examination room when called.

Most people are inherently fascinated by how things work, and **there are aspects of what you know and do in your business that the average**

person knows little about.

Perhaps you know something about a piece of equipment, a process, a skill, a body part or even something as dry as computer software. Whatever you think your customers don't know much about, solve the mystery for them.

To assist you in creating a meaningful video, imagine you are going to an elementary school to explain to children what you do for work. What are the "Did you know…?" statements you would share with them? If those same kids came to your office on a field trip, what would you show them first? These are your mysteries! Create videos about them.

If you have been in your business for more than a month, you have dozens of things you could discuss that others know little about. In my case, the video I wanted to create was about the workings of an eight-track tape and how it got its name. I have made many more similar mystery videos since with similar results.

By solving mysteries and sharing information in these videos, I not only engaged a group of people who were potential customers, but I established myself as an expert on the subject. This strategy increased my visibility on the YouTube channel and Google searches, and ultimately brought me more business.

WHAT TO DO:

- *Think of your institutional knowledge and find something that most people won't know. Think about those field trip items I mentioned.*
- *Set it up as a mystery with a question that starts with something like, "Do you know..."*
- *Set up a camera and film yourself showing it and talking about it.*
- *Make sure you have good audio and be personal.*
- *Add background music.*
- *Post the videos to your YouTube channel.*
- *Create a unique title for the video in the form of a question.*
- *Include the video on your web site along with text that can be generated by the video transcript. You can generate a great overview by putting the transcript of the video in an AI.*

MATCH INTERESTS

 Connect with potential customers using **common passions** and interests.

CORE CONCEPTS AND PRINCIPLES FOR SUCCESS:

- Create a personal connection with customers.
- Connect with a passionate audience.
- Generate low-pressure sales content.
- Build trust with potential customers.

If you run a business, you need to know your target audience. This means having a clear understanding of who you are trying to reach through your marketing and advertising.

I have three target markets: one for my recording studio, one for my consulting business, and one for Audiomover. Because Audiomover has two categories of projects, it has two distinct audiences:

1. **Organizational projects.** These projects are generally large and the target age for them is 35-50.
2. **Individual or family projects.** These projects are generally small and the target age for them is 51-70.

Audiomover's phone rings regularly with calls from 51-70 year old potential customers eager to discuss the tapes they want to digitize. These conversations often become nostalgic reflecting the interests and memories of those customers. We frequently end up talking about everything from classic movies and iconic music to our favorite TV shows. These are more than just business calls; they are trust-building windows into the past filled with common memories and cultural touchstones.

One day as I reflected on these interactions, inspiration struck. I went to my vast vinyl record collection and pulled out an old album by the band Styx. This particular album, "Paradise Theater," had a unique etching that created a mesmerizing rainbow effect when held up to the light. It was something many people from that era would be interested in.

I invited a friend over to my studio to discuss the album, its artwork, and the memories it evoked. While we talked, I recorded our conversation. As the cameras rolled, we discussed the music, delved into the nostalgia, and admired the amazing artwork. Naturally, I mentioned that we were recording this video in the Audiomover studios.

Much like strategy #4, the video wasn't a direct sales pitch about the services we offer. It was a genuine conversation, a shared experience, designed to connect with people who have similar interests and memories. The record itself had nothing to do with our services; it was simply a device that brought together people from a specific demographic.

When I uploaded the video to various platforms, including TikTok, I wasn't sure what to expect. To my amazement, it racked up close to 600,000 views on TikTok and thousands more on other platforms. The video introduced hundreds of thousands of people to Audiomover in a way that

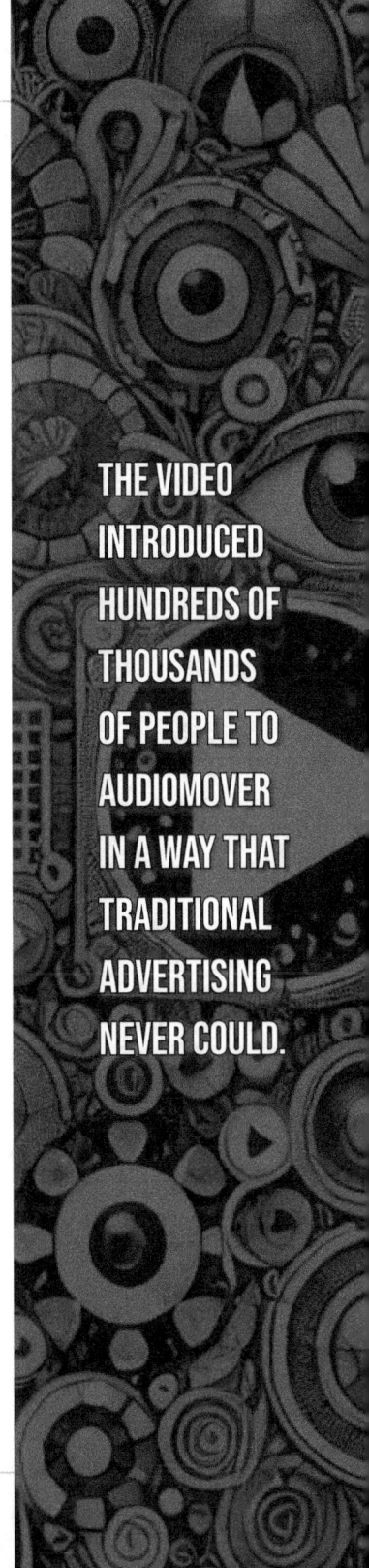

THE VIDEO INTRODUCED HUNDREDS OF THOUSANDS OF PEOPLE TO AUDIOMOVER IN A WAY THAT TRADITIONAL ADVERTISING NEVER COULD.

> THEN, SOMETHING TRULY REMARKABLE HAPPENED. THE PEOPLE MANAGING THEIR SOCIAL MEDIA POSTED THE VIDEO ON THEIR FACEBOOK PAGE WHICH OPENED US TO AN EVEN WIDER AUDIENCE.

traditional advertising never could.

It didn't surprise me that people in the older demographic responded positively to the video. On the other hand, what did surprise me was the number of young people who interacted with the video. They were vinyl collectors themselves, including one young person who created his own video and stitched it with our video. Although he was not in our target market, he did us a favor. He inadvertently spread our message to thousands more people.

Then, something truly remarkable happened. The people managing Styx's social media posted the video on their Facebook page which opened us to an even wider audience. And of course, most of these people were in our target demographic.

This experience taught me a valuable lesson: understanding and connecting with potential customers on a personal and emotional level is extremely valuable. Engaging with potential customers in meaningful ways drives them to you.

In this unlimited world of social media, the videos you make don't always have to be directly related to your business. Platforms like TikTok and tools like YouTube Shorts enable businesses to reach specific audiences by engaging them in content they are passionate about. Once they are engaged, it is easier to direct them to your website. This strategy not only expanded my reach but deepened my connection with my customers.

WHAT TO DO:

- *Consider the broad interests of your target market. Focus on their shared experiences, interests, cultural touchstones, even pop culture. Perhaps you have something interesting in your office that has little or nothing to do with your business.*
- *Film yourself talking about that shared memory or cultural touchstone. Use a prop if possible.*
- *Allow your passions and personality to come through.*
- *Encourage people to comment and share your video.*
- *Mention your business without doing a hard sell.*

GEO FOCUS

 *Reach new audiences by creating videos and media for specific regions.*

CORE CONCEPTS AND PRINCIPLES FOR SUCCESS:

- Benefit from location-based Google indexing.
- Find customers in under-served locations.
- Build trust with people in specific areas.
- Combine video and web page strategies.

Since the early days of Audiomover, packages have arrived daily from all over the country. As might be expected, our main sources of business are the heavily populated states - New York, Florida, and California - with Texas trailing not far behind.

One day, something unexpected happened. It started with a single order coming from Minnesota, a state known more for its lakes than its population. The next day, another order came in from Minnesota. And then another. Within a month, Minnesota was outpacing every other state in the quantity of orders. I found this sudden influx of orders from one of the least populated states both intriguing and perplexing.

Initially, I chalked it up to a local word-of-mouth phenomenon. Perhaps someone had shared our services on a neighborhood bulletin board, or maybe there was a community where everyone knew each other and had spread the word. This seemed plausible at first. But as the orders kept coming in, it became clear that something more significant was going on.

Determined to uncover the source of this mysterious boom, I delved into our web statistics. I noticed that our website was attracting a substantial amount of traffic from Minnesota, with search terms like "Cassette to CD Saint Paul" and "Minnesota cassette to CD." Intrigued by this, I searched further and discovered that all this traffic was converging on a single page.

When I pulled up that page, I scrutinized every detail. It was a standard order page on our site outlining our cassette-to-CD services. Nothing seemed out of the ordinary until I glanced at the right side of the page. There, I had placed a customer testimonial from someone in Saint Paul, MN. The testimonial was short and simple, but it included the customer's first name and their location - St. Paul, MN. And it was the only testimonial on the page.

This seemingly minor detail had a significant impact. Google, with its complex algorithms, had associated our services with Saint Paul, MN because of this single testimonial. The search engine saw our services, and "St. Paul, Minnesota," as interconnected entities, which resulted in a large amount of traffic going to that page. And if there was a company offering this service in St. Paul, we were suddenly stealing their customers.

The testimonial had another critical element: it was written in language used by the customer, not the jargon used by a tech professional. This obviously caught Google's attention and, subsequently, the attention of potential customers.

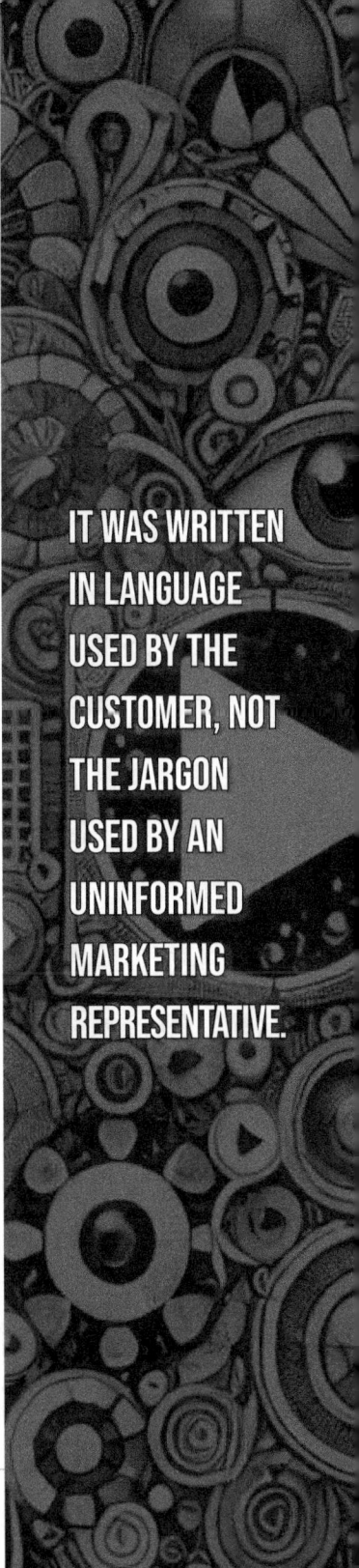

IT WAS WRITTEN IN LANGUAGE USED BY THE CUSTOMER, NOT THE JARGON USED BY AN UNINFORMED MARKETING REPRESENTATIVE.

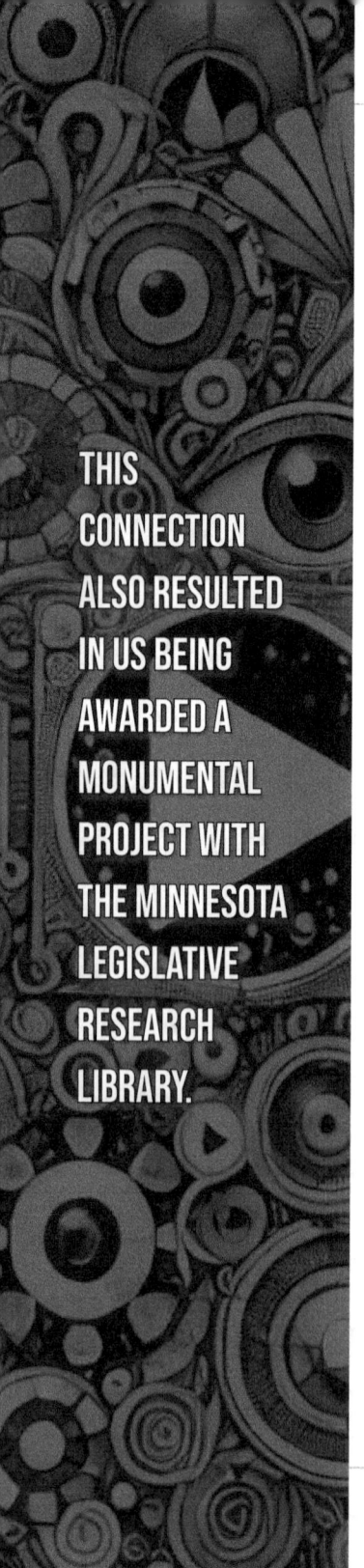

> THIS CONNECTION ALSO RESULTED IN US BEING AWARDED A MONUMENTAL PROJECT WITH THE MINNESOTA LEGISLATIVE RESEARCH LIBRARY.

The result was nothing short of astonishing and it led to something amazing. Not only were we buried with orders from Minnesota for several months, but this connection also resulted in us being awarded a monumental project submitted by the Minnesota Legislative Research Library. They hired us to digitize 28,000 cassette tapes and 2,000 reel-to-reel tapes - a task that kept our staff busy for an entire year. All of this stemmed from one customer testimonial that included a city and state.

This experience showed me the power of localized, customer-centric marketing. All you need to do is create a web page focused on specific cities or regions where your service is needed but not readily available, use testimonials written in the language of your customers, and tie those testimonials to specific locations.

When conducting web searches, identify areas where your services are lacking and draft pages dedicated to those areas. While results may vary, the rewards can be substantial. For us, a simple testimonial turned into a year's worth of business, proving that sometimes the smallest detail can lead to the greatest reward.

Do you have any testimonials from customers in under-served cities? Make a search-friendly page, even a video, dedicated to their location.

WHAT TO DO:

- *If possible, identify a market where your service is under represented.*
- *Create a page on your web site focused on a specific city, region or state. Use a testimonial if possible. Don't mix multiple locations together on a page. Be specific.*
- *Utilize text or a testimonial that is in the voice of a customer.*
- *Create a video about that specific location. Utilize a customer testimonial if possible. If not, just talk about the location. It would help if you have some knowledge or connection to it.*
- *Mention your business and invite viewers to utilize your product or service.*
- *Post the video to YouTube.*
- *Create a title that focuses on that location.*

7

WE'RE HERE

 *Grow your business by focusing on the local area.*

CORE CONCEPTS AND PRINCIPLES FOR SUCCESS:

- Reach customers who prefer to work with locals.
- Benefit from location-based Google indexing.
- Build trust with customers in a specific location.
- Combine video and web page strategies.

During the majority of the time Audiomover has been in business, we have not conducted any local marketing. Our primary service, which involves converting analog media to digital formats, has been conducted almost exclusively through the mail.

Audiomover's headquarters was in Denver, Colorado, for almost twenty years. During the first few years, it was in the basement of my home! Even so, I didn't put any effort into finding customers in the local market. We were only using our nation-wide, mail-based, business model.

Several years ago, a significant change occurred in my life. I wanted to leave the hustle and bustle of the big city and move to a quieter, warmer place. With that goal in mind, I moved Audiomover's headquarters to a small city in Southern Utah that was a fraction of the size of Denver.

Given that our business was conducted primarily through the mail, I figured moving the company would not have a negative impact on our business. Our operation was not dependent on a physical storefront or local clientele, so we could theoretically locate anywhere and maintain our nationwide presence.

So after settling in our new location, we added a few comments and references about our new home on our website. In a short time we started getting phone calls from locals wanting to drop off projects. These obscure references on our website started generating traffic in the local area. Amazingly, in the six years since relocating Audiomover to southern Utah, Audiomover has enjoyed a hundred times more local business than it ever did in Denver.

This statistic is even more amazing when you consider that our new location is in a warehouse district with no storefront.

This unexpected surge in local business taught me a valuable lesson. Regardless of whether your business operates on a national scale or a local scale, there's immense value in marketing to customers in your local area. There will always be a segment of the population that prefers the proximity of local businesses.

Here's the amazing part. Some of the local people we have worked with, haven't come to the studio, they have just sent their tapes to us through the mail. They simply felt more comfortable knowing that the business they were working with was theoretically down the street.

Over the past few years, I have wondered what would have happened if we had catered to customers located

IN THE SIX YEARS SINCE RELOCATING AUDIOMOVER, THE COMPANY HAS ENJOYED A HUNDRED TIMES MORE LOCAL BUSINESS THAN IT EVER DID IN DENVER.

> THE TRULY AMAZING PART WAS THAT EVEN SOME LOCALS USE THE MAIL TO SEND THEIR TAPES. THERE WAS SOMETHING ABOUT THE PROXIMITY THAT ADDED AN EXTRA LEVEL OF TRUST AND COMFORT.

in the Denver area. We might have been swimming in tapes from locals. This realization underscores the importance of doing local marketing.

It's important to remember there's a segment of the population that prefers working with local businesses. Even if your primary operation is nationwide and conducted through the mail, never underestimate the importance of local marketing. It's a simple yet powerful way to expand your reach.

It's likely you have a page on your web site with your location and contact information. But you can do more. Make a page dedicated to your local area. Include some photos of the area. Mention places you like and even make a video talking about why you love the city and state you live in.

If you are a nationwide business, don't overlook sending a message to locals. And if you are a locally-focused business, make a page and some videos dedicated to your area. Not sales videos, just videos about where you are located and why.

So even if your business isn't built for local access, don't overlook the potential customers in your area. You might be leaving money on the table. There are customers that will seek out your products and services simply because of the proximity.

WHAT TO DO:

- *Create a page on your web site focused on the local area.*
- *Record a video talking about the city you are based in and the places you love in the area.*
- *Load the video to YouTube.*
- *Create a title that has keywords related to the local area.*
- *Embed the video on your local page on your web site.*

8

FAQ = SALES PITCH

How to turn your FAQ page into a marketing resource.

CORE CONCEPTS AND PRINCIPLES FOR SUCCESS:

- Create search-friendly content.
- Learn what people want by studying search trends.
- Generate media that acts as a soft sell.
- Combine utilitarian needs and marketing.

To run a business, you must wear many hats, and one of those hats is ensuring high-quality customer service. This often means spending time on the phone answering questions. Over the years at Audiomover, I frequently found myself answering the same questions over and over. Customers text, message, and call asking about our services. After answering the same questions hundreds of times, my answers became clearer.

Like most companies, to address this issue, I created a Frequently Asked Questions (FAQ) page on our website. On this page, I compiled the most commonly asked questions and provided clear, concise answers to those questions. Obviously, this enables customers to find the information they need without having to call or text us.

But even though the FAQ page is a valuable resource, these pages won't satisfy every customer's needs. Many people are impatient and will not take the time to read our FAQ page. And some people want to hear a voice. As a result, many still call or text us looking for a quick answer.

There is also a very large group of people who utilize a different tactic altogether. Rather than scouring through the FAQ on a company page or attempting to communicate directly, they will go to Google and do a search there. I am one of those people. This tactic frequently helps me find the answer I'm looking for much more quickly than perusing the company's FAQ page.

This got me thinking, if I made a video for my FAQs, I could answer the questions, benefit from speed of Google search results, and add a personal touch at the same time. So rather than relying exclusively on a FAQ page, I decided to use our FAQs as topics to create videos that engage our customers on a personal level.

I took the questions customers asked most often, sat down in front of a camera and answered them clearly and distinctly. The videos were conversational, engaging and informative and gave customers a sense of who I am and what Audiomover is all about.

We posted the videos on YouTube as well as our website and other social media channels. Customers could watch them and feel like they were having a one-on-one conversation with me. They also knew they were receiving answers from someone who was knowledgeable and passionate about the topic.

This approach enabled customers to get the information they were seeking without having to call or text us. For those customers who did not have the

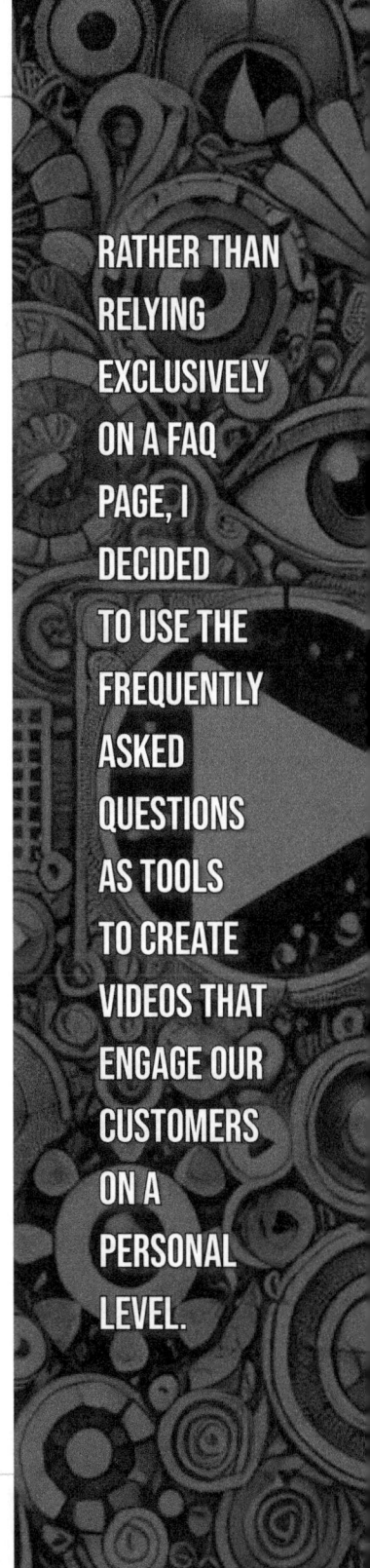

RATHER THAN RELYING EXCLUSIVELY ON A FAQ PAGE, I DECIDED TO USE THE FREQUENTLY ASKED QUESTIONS AS TOOLS TO CREATE VIDEOS THAT ENGAGE OUR CUSTOMERS ON A PERSONAL LEVEL.

patience to read through a FAQ page, these videos were a perfect alternative.

I also added some pleasant background music to the videos. This created an element of comfort and emotion a phone call or text can't provide.

Unexpectedly, these videos did more than just answer questions; they turned our FAQ into a soft sales tool. Our FAQ videos became easily discoverable on search engines for a wide variety of searches. The YouTube transcripts were keyword-heavy, the titles were specific and search engine friendly, and the customers got to know me as a person. So not only did we post the videos on our YouTube channel, we also posted them on our web site.

Believe it or not, many customers have told us they watched our FAQ videos before deciding to use our services. This feedback reinforces the value of FAQ videos and shows how effective they can be in building trust and confidence with customers.

I found it beneficial to check out our competitors' FAQ pages to see what questions they were addressing. This helped me expand our own list of questions and create an even more comprehensive video library.

In the end, these videos didn't just reduce the number of phone calls and texts coming into our office, they helped our customers get to know us in a way that felt personal and genuine.

Creating a library of FAQ videos not only saved time and energy for the company, it became an unexpected sales tool that continues to pay dividends even years later. In our case, because the videos didn't require any visuals, they were easy to produce. And because of the quantity of potential questions, whether frequently asked or not, we had a massive supply of content that could be placed on any platform and reused regularly.

Creating FAQ videos turned a typical business problem into a powerful marketing tool.

WHAT TO DO:

- *Make a list of your FAQs.*
- *Create a separate video for each question, even if it is only a few seconds long. You can also create one long video that contains all of the questions or groups of questions. Each can be a separate piece of content.*

- *State the question at the beginning of the video. Even put it on screen if possible.*
- *Add background music.*
- *Post the videos to your YouTube channel and the FAQ page on your web site.*
- *Create titles for each video that match the question exactly.*

9

REACT

 *How you can utilize the popularity of reaction videos as a soft seller.*

CORE CONCEPTS AND PRINCIPLES FOR SUCCESS:

- Utilize content that is already successful.
- Showcase your passion to attract people.
- Build trust as an expert.
- Showcase your personality.

Reaction videos have become a significant phenomenon in the world of media. People from all walks of life record themselves watching content and their reactions to it. This engaging format has taken the world by storm over the last decade. The question now is, can this strategy be harnessed to boost your business?

There are countless types of reaction videos: people reacting to news stories, music videos, movie clips, TED talks, and many more. These videos attract viewers who enjoy watching genuine, unscripted reactions to content they love and/or are curious about.

Many of my marketing customers see the potential of reaction videos but have no idea how to use them effectively in their business.

But it's easier than you think.

Some time ago I was watching an interview with Neil deGrasse Tyson, a well-known astrophysicist. He explained that when he watched the movie "Titanic" he noticed that there was something wrong. He went on to explain that when he met James Cameron, the director of "Titanic," Tyson informed him that the position of the starry sky in the end of the movie was incorrect. The position of the stars was wrong based on the historical date and location of the Titanic's sinking. In other words, Tyson had unique knowledge about something in the movie that almost no one else would have noticed.

Thousands, perhaps millions, of people were fascinated by Tyson's insight in this interview. And although he didn't create a reaction video, this is an ideal example of something you could do for your business.

Whatever your business is, there's a strong possibility there has been something in a movie or TV show that relates to what you do. This could be a scene involving someone in your profession, a piece of equipment, or a situation. For example, you could create a reaction video showing you watching a scene from a movie and explaining why it's accurate or inaccurate.

If you operate a car repair shop, you might find a scene in an action movie showing a high-speed car chase. You could point out the parts of the car chase that are realistic and those that are Hollywood fiction. Or you might find something less exciting like a scene in a tire shop. You could talk about the tires in the background, the visible tools, the types of cars used in a scene, or repair shops in general.

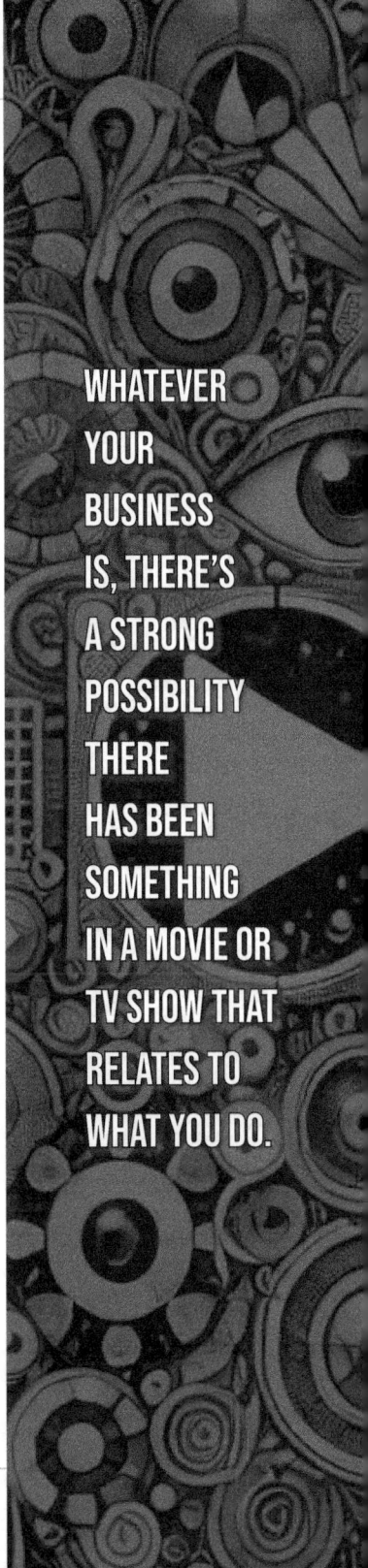

WHATEVER YOUR BUSINESS IS, THERE'S A STRONG POSSIBILITY THERE HAS BEEN SOMETHING IN A MOVIE OR TV SHOW THAT RELATES TO WHAT YOU DO.

YOU HAVE INSTITUTIONAL KNOWLEDGE THAT CAN BE USED TO CREATE ENGAGING CONTENT THAT CAN DIRECT PEOPLE TO YOUR BUSINESS AND BUILD TRUST.

This will not only entertain your audience, it will showcase your expertise in your professional area.

If you're in the medical field, you could talk about scenes from a popular medical TV show, discuss the accuracy of the procedures shown, and point out the realism of the environment. You could also talk about the way medical professionals are portrayed. Your insights will be valuable to those viewers who are curious about the reality of what they are watching.

Any reaction video you create can also be used as a springboard to highlight your knowledge and personality. If the content you choose to discuss is popular, it will help draw viewers to your video. The combination of familiar content with expert commentary can be very engaging. And connecting yourself with something popular can dramatically increase your reach.

Between movies, TV shows and other YouTube videos, there are probably thousands of clips that relate in some way to your business.

If reacting to a movie or video seems too daunting, find a news story instead. Chances are there is an article or blog post that has come out in the recent past that you could read and comment on. Just search Google news. You could even conduct a search on some legacy newspapers or magazines and do commentary on that.

The point is, you have institutional knowledge that can be used to create engaging content. That content can direct people to your business, build trust in the eyes or your potential customers and increase your visibility to search engines.

WHAT TO DO:

- *Find a movie scene, a TV show or YouTube video that includes a topic or location you are knowledgeable about.*
- *Locate a news story that involves some area of expertise.*
- *Set up a camera and record yourself reacting to the video or news story. Stop throughout and point out important things you notice. Especially things that people not familiar with the industry would miss.**
- *Speak directly to the camera and allow your personality to come out.*
- *Post the video to YouTube.*

- *Create a title that is engaging and relates to the piece of content you are reacting to.*

*Reaction videos can be technically challenging and may require additional hardware and software.

PLEASE NOTE: This chapter is not intended to give you any legal advice. Consult an attorney when creating videos that include copyrighted content. There may be restrictions as to what you can and cannot use to create a reaction video. Be sure to obtain permission when necessary.

IT'S JUST ME

 *Connect with customers by **telling stories** and **interviewing yourself**.*

CORE CONCEPTS AND PRINCIPLES FOR SUCCESS:

- Create large quantities of short-form content.
- Utilize the eavesdropping principle.
- Capitalize on people's love of stories.
- Generate large quantities of content easily.

Podcasts are everywhere. They are a powerful tool for broadcasting messages, sharing stories, and connecting with audiences on a more personal level. They offer far more than just being a platform for discussion. For savvy business owners, podcasts are a treasure trove of content that can be used for creative marketing. Everything you say in a podcast, from a six second statement to a ten minute story, can be used as a piece of content.

One afternoon around 2017 when I was browsing YouTube, I saw a short video that caught my attention. The video featured a charismatic individual passionately discussing his business philosophies. He was sitting at a table in what looked like a studio. He appeared to be on a podcast talking to someone. Curiously, I neither saw nor heard the interviewer. This absence sparked the following question: Is it possible that clip wasn't actually taken from an interview? Is it possible that no one was actually interviewing this person? How would I know without seeing an entire show or a much longer clip?

Recognizing the strategic value of podcast clips, and inspired by those questions, I created my own mock podcast. I located a comfortable corner in our studio where I could create a professional podcast look. I arranged the lights, positioned the microphones, and set up the cameras. Then, I took a seat and began answering questions and talking to a phantom host. The cameras rolled as I delved into the history of my business, described the services we offer, and explained our purpose and philosophy. It was an interview without an interviewer - a perfect illusion.

Why did I go through all this effort, you might ask? The answer is simple: control, convenience and eavesdropping. Many podcasts have limited audiences, and not all viewers will be interested in the message you want to communicate. By creating a mock podcast, you retain complete control of the narrative. You decide what aspects of your story you want to highlight and how to present them.

You can also film the podcast at your convenience, eliminating the hassle and technical issues of coordinating a podcast interview.

And finally, eavesdropping. One of the reasons the TV talk show format became successful in the first place was the eavesdropping element. The host and guest never look at the camera so the audience feels as though they are listening in on a private conversation. It's subtle but powerful.

Once the recording was complete, I had a mountain of content ready to use. Each question I answered became a stand-alone video, perfect for

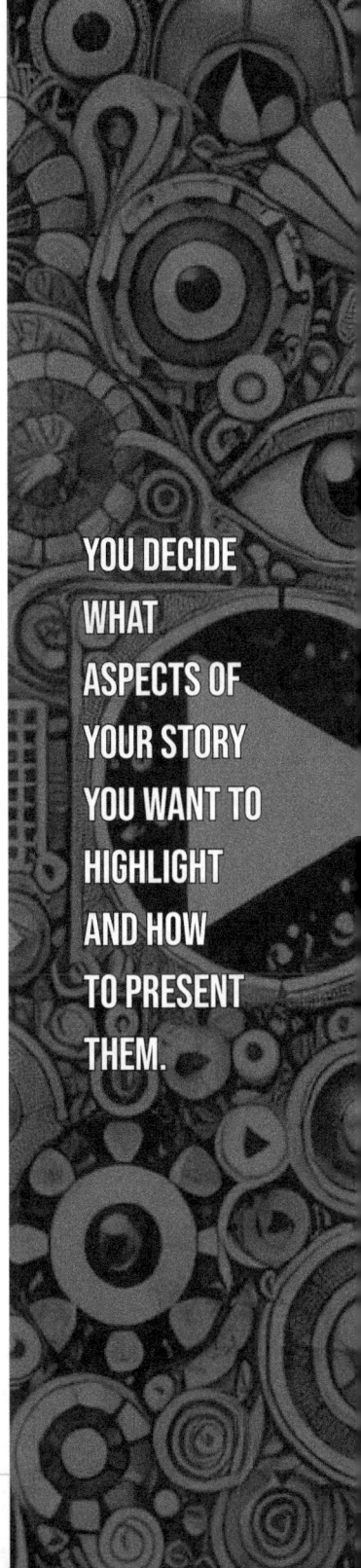

YOU DECIDE WHAT ASPECTS OF YOUR STORY YOU WANT TO HIGHLIGHT AND HOW TO PRESENT THEM.

> EVERY PODCAST SEGMENT CAN BE A POWERFUL MARKETING TOOL, EVERY CLIP CAN BECOME A STANDALONE VIDEO, AND EVERY ANSWER TO A QUESTION CAN BECOME A PROMOTIONAL PIECE.

posting on our YouTube channel and social media platforms. The process was seamless, efficient, and incredibly effective.

And then I took it a step further. Rather than just responding to questions about my business, I used it as a way to tell my story.

If you've ever been to a live presentation, whether it's a business summit, a sales seminar or even a church meeting, you will notice that people become more engaged whenever the presenter shares a story. So I took the opportunity to tell stories about my business. I shared the events that led to the start of my business, told stories about the really interesting projects we've worked on, and described the impactful learning experiences I've had.

Again, this mock podcast allowed me to have complete control of the entire process and get the results that I wanted.

Of course there's nothing wrong with

following the traditional route of being a guest on someone else's podcast. This can be highly effective. There are tens of thousands of podcast hosts seeking interesting people to interview. Have one of your team members research relevant podcasts and talk to them about featuring you. These appearances can provide valuable content you can use on your own marketing channels.

Whether you choose to create a mock podcast or be interviewed by hosts with their own podcasts, keep in mind the following takeaways. Every podcast segment you create can be a powerful marketing tool. Every clip can become a standalone video. And every answer to a question can become a promotional piece. All you need to do is set up your microphone, position your camera, and start recording.

The next time you think about podcasting, remember: it's not just about getting your message out to potential customers. It's about creating rich content that can be used and reused for years.

WHAT TO DO:

- *Make a list of questions you would like to answer if you were on a podcast.*
- *Rehearse the details of stories about your business, its origins and interesting experiences you have had along the way.*
- *Set up a camera and record yourself answering questions and telling stories.*

- *Do NOT look at the camera. This is an eavesdropping illusion.*
- *Create a unique video for the answer to each question.*
- *Generate unique titles for each video that feature the question you are answering.*
- *Put the transcript of each video in an AI and use it as a written overview or as the foundation for a blog.*

THE BOOK

 *How to use print on demand tools to **create a book** as a marketing tool.*

CORE CONCEPTS AND PRINCIPLES FOR SUCCESS:

- Gain credibility as the author of a book.
- Use POD to create a book with no investment.
- Distribute a book as a marketing strategy.
- Rethink the broad definition of "book" today.

In 2019, I was doing some historical research for a project at our studio. I was sifting through some old scanned newspapers, searching for articles on a specific topic. As I delved into early 1900s publications, I kept stumbling on articles about a disease called the Spanish Influenza. At the time, I had never heard of it and didn't know what it was, but my curiosity was piqued. I started archiving those articles, planning to read more about the disease at a later time.

Fast forward to March 2020. COVID-19 disrupted our lives and suddenly, everyone was talking about pandemics. This jogged my memory of the Spanish Influenza articles I had found. It occurred to me that there was probably a large audience of people who would love to read these articles.

Because of their age, these articles were in the public domain and there were no copyright restrictions. So rather than just post them to a website, I investigated the process of creating a book. And I was shocked at the ease of publishing a book today.

The articles were faded and difficult to read, so I meticulously re-wrote them in a Word document. I then created an introduction to each article explaining where I found it and describing the historical setting.

Next, I put the articles and introductions together. Each combination became its own chapter. I gathered graphics from the newspapers, created a nice graphic for the cover and ultimately created a book titled Virus 1918 and sold it on Amazon.

From the moment I had the idea to the moment is was published was two weeks. To my surprise, it sold extremely well, and generated a nice profit for me.

The first thing I would like you to ask yourself is, what is a book? Of course it can be a paperback you have on your shelf. But today it's also an electronic document you read on your kindle app, or even that audiobook you listen to on your mobile device.

Now ask yourself, how is that eBook different than a blog? How is that audiobook different than a podcast? The only difference is in your mind. Any rules and limitations are completely made up.

Theoretically, you could take the last email you wrote and publish it as a book on Amazon this week. Again, all the rules you attach to writing a book are completely in your head. So consider the almost unlimited possibilities.

YOU COULD TAKE THE LAST EMAIL YOU WROTE AND PUBLISH IT AS A BOOK ON AMAZON THIS WEEK.

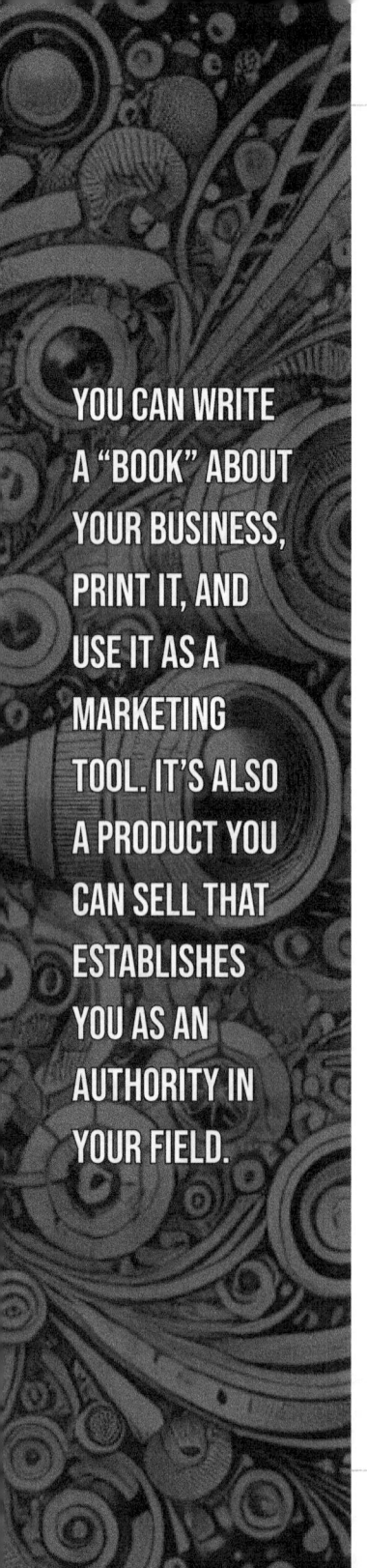

> YOU CAN WRITE A "BOOK" ABOUT YOUR BUSINESS, PRINT IT, AND USE IT AS A MARKETING TOOL. IT'S ALSO A PRODUCT YOU CAN SELL THAT ESTABLISHES YOU AS AN AUTHORITY IN YOUR FIELD.

Creating a book is a lot easier than you might think. And believe it or not, it costs nothing to produce.

Creating my book introduced me to a powerful tool for entrepreneurs: Amazon's Kindle Direct Publishing (KDP). KDP enables you to publish electronic and printed books without any upfront cost. All you need to do is set up a KDP account, load your Word document, and within a few days your electronic book will be available for purchase on Amazon. It costs you nothing to do this, and every time someone buys your book or reads a few pages of it, you earn royalties.

For the printed version you will have to put forth a little more effort to set up the margins, the front and back covers, etc., but Amazon handles the printing and shipping using a Print-On-Demand (POD) model. Using this model, no physical copies are made until they are ordered. As a result, you can publish your book without spending a dime, and get royalties from book sales every month.

Using KDP as a publisher was a game-changer for me, and I've used it several times since. In fact, the book you are currently reading was originally published using KDP.

One of the other benefits of KDP is that it allows you to order "author copies" for a few dollars each. With this feature you could write a "book" about your business, order as many author copies as you need, and give them away as a marketing tool. And because it would also be available for purchase on Amazon, being a published author establishes you as an authority in your field.

When I discuss the "book printing" possibility with some customers it sounds daunting at first. But remember, the rules of a "book" are all in your head. A book does not have to be long. It doesn't have to represent your life's work.

But why stop with printed books? You can create audiobooks as well. Creating audiobooks isn't complicated and you can publish them for free on dozens of platforms including Audible, Barnes & Noble, and even public libraries. Services like Findaway Voices distribute your audiobook to numerous platforms, earning you royalties every time someone downloads your Audiobook or borrows it from a library.*

Utilizing the KDP self-publishing strategy, you can create valuable marketing tools that elevate your brand, highlight your expertise, and enable you to reach a wider audience - all without having to spend any money. It's a powerful strategy for entrepreneurs looking to expand their reach and influence.

Naturally, you can step it up with a little more effort. You can add graphics, do interesting formatting, create a nice cover, etc. The point here is, the barrier of entry is almost non existent. It's a powerful tool with a broad range of applications. You are only limited by your willingness to do it.

Don't think of a book as your life's work or a massive undertaking. Anything you write can become a book.

WHAT TO DO:

- *Write something, or gather things you've already written.*
- *Organize it in a Word document.*
- *Create a KDP account with Amazon.*
- *Upload your document and use the built in KDP tools to create a cover.*
- *Once you have done this, you are for all intents and purposes ready to publish your eBook.*
- *From here KDP will give you instructions on how to publish the paperback version.*

* An audiobook will need to meet some specific audio specifications that may require an audio professional. But almost any basic recording studio should be able to help. Once completed you can load it directly to Audible using acx.com and to numerous other platforms using a distributer like findawayvoices.com.

CONTACT

Thank you for taking the time to read this book. I hope it has been helpful.

I am available for **consulting,** and my businesses are available to help with **media work**. We can help you develop and implement any of the ideas in this book or any other audio/video or marketing initiatives you have in mind.

Reach me through my marketing firm at **thickandmystic.com** or my personal web site **robertjohnhadfield.com.**

You can also reach me at Utah South Studios **(435) 703-6529.**

www.ingramcontent.com/pod-product-compliance
Lightning Source LLC
Chambersburg PA
CBHW071938210526
45479CB00002B/725